*Burnt Offerings*

*Burnt Offerings*

# "BURNT OFFERINGS"

Copyright 1996 by Gail Smith and Janet Hastings

All rights reserved. Printed in the United States of America. No part of this book may be used or reproduced in any manner whatsoever without written permission except in the case of brief quotations embodied in critical articles and reviews.

All activities, and consequences thereof, resulting from performing the "BURNT OFFERINGS" ritual are the sole responsibility of the intended user. Caution should be used to ignite matches, paper, incense, and candles. Do not leave any of these items unattended at any time. The authors assume no responsibility for the actions of the user.

copyright registered (#TXU876-105).
"BURNT OFFERINGS" WGA Reg. #'s 714065, 710084, & 756370.

ISBN  0-615-13327-4

Editing and book layout by Philip E. Foster
Computer and graphic design by Geoffrey Frank
Cover photography by Ryan Severin
2006 revised graphics and layout by Ray Moran
Correspondence to the authors can be communicated via email at:
www.myspace.com/burntofferingsbook

# A Postscript to our Readers

Often, it is in retrospect that we see something in our creations that we didn't see in them initially. Over time, they reveal hidden aspects, and deeper meanings that weren't obvious to us at their inception.

When we wrote BURNT OFFERINGS ten years ago, we were unaware that what we were presenting to people was a form of alchemy -- the process of changing one substance into another through the heat of the fire. The ancient alchemists not only used this process to turn lead into gold, but they also used it spiritually to refine and purify their souls. It is only through this alchemical process of burning away the dross of selfishness, greed and hate, that we can emerge a more integrated and evolved soul.

Through the years of working with BURNT OFFERINGS, we realized that a much larger concept was taking form. We realized that just living life is part of the process of refining the soul. Our decisions form a basis for our reality, and as we deal with the outcomes of our decisions we grow and develop into more complete people. We had no agenda when we wrote BURNT OFFERINGS, other than to help others look at their problems and challenges in a different way, so that the burden of worry and anxiety could be lifted by a change in energy and consciousness. Also, learning to "know thyself," gives life a new excitement and wonder because you understand yourself better, and this opens up a new world of "infinite possibilities."

Anyone who graciously accepts life's ups and downs, and uses them to learn and grow is a modern alchemist. Like the phoenix, who burns himself down into ashes, and then rises-up more beautiful then before, so does the alchemist re-evaluate his life, and then lets go of everything that no longer serves him. He forgives old hurts and adversaries, and moves forward into a new life full of light and promise.

When you accept the truth of change, you learn that each season has a beauty and a purpose. Death is just another season, a change into a different vibration. By losing the heaviness of the body and ego, you are freer and lighter, and can dwell on things of the spirit instead of the material. If and when you choose to return to earth you will have gone through a refinement process of elevating your soul to a higher level. This is the never-ending process of life after life.

We were given visions and dreams that we could have ignored, but spirit was tenacious, and we knew we had to research deeper into ourselves, and into history, and sacred places to make the connections on our own sacred journey. When a publisher asked us to write three chapters about this journey, it sent us on a long and involved trip through many unusual experiences and fascinating people. The three chapters grew into a complete book called THE BEST JOURNEYS HAVE NO DESTINATIONS, that will be available in 2006-2007.

When we desire to evolve into something greater, we open up a pathway into a richer, more developed life, where we live with courage, honor and respect for others. We can live in peace and harmony with one another, and we can heal the planet, but it has to begin with each individual taking responsibility for his life and his actions. There is great strength in kindness and compassion and love, but they have to be lived, and used so we can evolve into a more elevated society.

We hope that when you use BURNT OFFERINGS, the power of the purifying fire reveals the "alchemical gold" inherent in your very being.

# DEDICATION

For our children, our beacons of light for the future.

Bob

Matthew

Stephanie

Heather

Kristen

Tricia

May they find their God-given gifts to assist them through their lives, and may they share these gifts with all who seek the path of enlightenment.

# Acknowledgements

To our wonderful husbands, Glenn Smith and Tom Hastings, for believing in us and our ideas. Their scientific and educational backgrounds are a source of grounding. They have kept their minds open to the realms of possibilities and unexplainable phenomena that we have experienced during the research and development of this project. We thank them for their unconditional support and for their encouragement to share our ideas with the world.

Many thanks to all of our friends and colleagues who have encouraged us, and to everyone who has believed in this project. Special thanks to:

Valerie Bagot

Joanne Cohen

Philip E Foster

Dario Mazzoli

John Nicoletti

Sharlette Schwenninger

Dona St. Hill

John Zenone

...for being there at the beginning and supporting us to the end.

To our Readers...

We never dreamed this project would take us down so many paths of learning and knowledge, but by reading and investigating history and ancient lore, we stepped into a whole new world, that awakened many past life memories. These memories have great relevance in our lives today.

Learn to "know thyself," and in this process you will learn your strengths an weaknesses, which will allow you to know others in love and compassion. When you chart your Burnt Offerings in the journal section of this book, you are really charting your sacred journey. (Notice the similarity of journal and journey). Take note of the synchronicities and spiritual signposts, and use them wisely. Also, don't forget to laugh and have fun — life is meant to be joyful.

Godspeed to you on your journey, and perhaps we will meet as pilgrims on the path to enlightenment.

Blessings in Love and Light.

# Table of Contents

Dedication.................................................................1
Acknowledgements...................................................2
To Our Readers.........................................................3
Table of Contents......................................................4
Opening Statement....................................................5
Ritual......................................................................6-8
BURNT OFFERINGS Preface..............................9-11
"The Fire is Lit"..................................................12-15
Contents of Ritual....................................................16
Centering.............................................................17-18
The Beginning.....................................................19-20
Symbols....................................................................21
Affirmations: .....................................................22-52

    Love* Friendship* Happiness*
    Self-confidence* Sexuality* Marriage*
    Creating a Baby* Birth of a Baby*
    Success* Travel* Universal* Protection*
    School & Learning* Relationship-Beginning*
    Relationship-Ending* Deployment of
    a Loved One* Inheritance* Wealth*
    Prejudice* Religion* Loneliness* Abuse*
    Addiction* Eating Disorder* Aging*
    Surgery* Losing a Job* Personality Conflict*
    Guilt* Shame*

Prayers-    Universal* For the Dying* Peace*    53-56
Spiritual Vocabulary..................................................57-60
Self-help Suggestions: Alphabetized, Addiction-Wealth 61-91
Journal......................................................................92-101

# Opening Statement

"Burnt Offerings" provides simple and practical tools along with a sacred ritual that will effortlessly take you on a journey into spirituality and self-awareness.

It is a unique, millennium approach to solving problems by blending ancient and modern concepts of spirituality. If you apply the ritual, it has the power to change your life and ignite your soul.

Because of its universal message of love, hope and self-improvement, it can be applied to any human experience, challenge or problem.

Our sincere hope is that "Burnt Offerings" empowers you to improve the quality of your life by easing your burdens, which will allow you to move forward to a place of peace, contentment and fulfillment.

"Burnt Offerings" is the inter-relationship between God and Man — give up your burdens to God through the power of the sacred fire.

# Ritual

a ceremony, established forms, a system of rites, a formality, a customary or regular practice, (from Latin r(Etus).

Webster's Dictionary

# *Life is a ritual...*

... Almost everyone has a morning routine, whether it's having a cup of coffee and reading the morning paper or exercising and drinking a health drink, these everyday routines are rituals, and they give us a sense of order and grounding to our lives. Some of our more elaborate rituals include weddings, funerals, the Catholic Mass, Bar mitzvahs, etc. These meaningful occasions use a system of rites that bring reverence to a special place in time to all who participate in them.

All great civilizations have worshipped their own Gods, using a ritual to connect more closely with their Gods. For instance, the North American Indians during their sacred rain dances used specific dance steps to the beat of special drumming, wearing ceremonial feathers and garments. They believed that following each step of the ritual in mind and soul assured a deep communication with the Great Spirit.

We, in today's world, can use sacred ritual to still ourselves long enough for our souls to touch a higher power. When this happens we feel energy and a sense of joy and contentment; while any stressful or fearful emotions that have been living in our psyches are released to the universe. For most, this is the beginning of a powerful journey leading to an awakening of spirit, and a more profound connection to their fellow man.

Embracing the ritual of "BURNT OFFERINGS" and having faith that it can change your life can help guide you along your chosen path.

".. and Abraham said, my son, God will provide himself a lamb for a BURNT OFFERINGS: so they went both of them together."

Genesis 22:-8

# "Believe that fire is God's sacred gift"

"BURNT OFFERINGS" is a universal ritual that can be used by all people, for we are all born facing the same sun, breathing the same air and walking the same earth. Open your heart and accept the similarities as well as the differences, growing in love for yourself and the universe. By the way we live our lives in truth, fairness and compassion is a message of acceptance and love to all mankind. Treat your fellow man as you wish to be treated.

The Following statement came to Gail from spirit, during deep prayer in 1996

> *"Prejudice shall be the ruination of man. The only reason I gave the differences were for spice and flavor, and man has taken it to the far extent."*

**World peace can become possible through respecting each others traditions, values and faiths.**

As human beings we have been given the unique gift of free will, enabling us to taste and savor all the wonders and mysteries of this infinite universe. With this free will comes the acceptance and responsibility of the universal law of cause and effect. Our choices under this law create the tones and paths of our lives. We have been told to walk the path and grow, lighting the way for others and ourselves. "BURNT OFFERINGS" is a tool for this journey, helping you to tap into that quiet space in your heart, to the spot where goodness and love dwell. Your soul or your light, whichever you choose to call it, is a place of wonder where all things are possible through divine and spiritual healing. This is where your light and the light of God blend to become pure energy, an energy filled with understanding, wisdom and awareness of the complex and sometimes trying times of our lives.

The light may come in the birth of a grand idea or in a vision that pulsates with beauty before your eyes, or in a flood of awareness, emotion and love, or a deep oneness with the universe. This journey of light brings you closer to the center of your existence and an acceptance and love FOR WHO YOU ARE — you must learn to love yourself before you can give love to others.

Think of the joy you feel when two like souls come together. Think of the deep happiness you feel when your heart connects with a new friend or lover. This special bond makes us feel more complete and content with our place in this vast and sometimes confusing world. However, for some, the solitary journey is the correct journey, affording the greatest growth and life lessons.

By bringing forth this ancient practice of purification, meditation and prayer, you set time and space aside to ask for help in your time of need. This method will become a tool to advance your dreams and enrich your experience in life. Realize that all things can take many shapes, forms and degrees of importance; after you perform "BURNT OFFERINGS" your problem may not be cured, but the significance of it will change.

For instance, you might remove your energy from it causing the circumstances around it to shift; or you might adjust your attitude and feelings so that the power around the problem weakens and dissipates.

Faith is a very important part of change. If you have faith along with some practical guidelines, solutions and changes will come forth. If you listen, and have faith in the process, your inner voice from that quiet place of love and light will speak to you and you will receive an answer.

Moving along the path of enlightenment is the greatest gift we give ourselves. Rejoice in love for all things and pass the light freely to your fellow man.

"THE FIRE IS LIT
TO DRAW SPIRIT
TO THE PROBLEM AND SOURCE."

*Fire* was one of the most sacred gifts that God gave to primitive man to lighten his dark world. That phenomena of light and flame illuminated his caves, cooked his food and gave him warmth. As man progressed, fire became more than just a tool, it became a sacred symbol, a divine gift. The ancient Vedic scriptures from India say that Agni, or fire, is the messenger between people and their Gods, and ashes were called the seed of Agni, from which its followers would be reborn. In modern Brahman home today, they still keep sacred fires burning. The Aztecs and Mayans also worshipped Gods of fire with sacred flames, ignited by the sun's rays using concave, metallic mirrors. The Zoroastrians believe that fire is the earthly representative of the Sun, the giver of all life.

In the early Middle Ages in Europe, the Teutonic and Slav peoples had fire festivals called "need-fire" These "need-fires" were built during epidemics of cattle disease and plagues, and were considered the only sure remedy. After the fires had died-down, the people would cover themselves in the ashes for purification and protection, and would not remove the ashes for many days.

The worship of the divine, the holy, has always been hallowed by the light of fire, from the ancient Hebrews with their lamps of sacred oil for the worship of Yehweh, to the Catholic Church and their wax candles carried by their "light bearers" The ancient Assyrians would light a torch from a sacred fire then carry it through the town lighting other sacred fires, thus "carrying the torch for the divine." This tradition is carried out today with the lighting of the Olympic torch a the Olympic games, signifying unity and brotherhood.

Also, almost all peoples have their own "Festival of Lights." The Jews have Hanukkah, and in England there is Candlemas Day, feast of the purification of Mary. Similar festivals take place in India, Tibet and Thailand.

In many great religions through the ages, incense has been burned as a prayer or an offering that rises up through the smoke to the sacred realms.

The ancient Egyptians used incense in all of their sacred temples dedicated to Ra, the Sun God, or Isis and Osiris and many other deities, as a means of purification and prayer, as did the Jews, Buddhists, and later the Christians.

One of the most powerful symbols in relationship to "BURNT OFFERINGS" is the Phoenix, the mythical bird of fire that resurrects itself out of its own ashes. In the Egyptian religion, this eagle-like, purple and gold bird would come out of Arabia or India to Heliopolis to build its nest on the altar of the Sun God; it would then be consumed by fire and rise again from the ashes young and beautiful. Thus, the Phoenix has become the symbol of resurrection and immortality the world over.

One of the most recognizable symbols in the world is the pyramid, or triangular shape, from the Greek, meaning spirit, thought or idea of fire. The shape represented a volcanic cone recalling Fire Mountains. The upward leap of the flames toward heaven is another popular meaning of the fire pyramid as well. "BURNT OFFERINGS" brings these same sacred properties to modern man so that he can change his world and bring enlightenment and knowledge to all situations. Use this ritual of purification and cleansing to ease your burdens and light the way to a higher consciousness. As the fire burns in the pan, it ignites the spiritual fire in your soul. As you meditate on the burning ashes, picture the Phoenix taking your burdens on its fiery wings up to the heavens toward the central Sun, to God. This lifting of the burden will leave a void in your psyche, an opening to receive; and since nothing is ever wasted in the universe, whatever negative energy you release to a higher power, will be transmuted into positive energy in the form of creative fire. This positive energy will "build a fire" under the foundation of your life and lead you to a more authentic way of being. Feel the fire in your heart that spreads its light to a greater awareness, and move forth to create positive changes.

## Contents of the ritual

"BURNT OFFERINGS" is recommended for individuals 18 years of age and older. (Individuals under 18 years of age must have adult supervision).

Each "BURNT OFFERINGS" ritual kit should contain the following:

1. Container (i.e., box, pouch, etc.)
2. Burner (i.e., metal, stone, etc., or any non-flammable substance)
3. Small papers (approximately 1x2 inches)
4. Incense cones
5. Pen
6. Candle (white)
7. Touchstone (i.e., a crystal or stone that feels comfortable in your hand)

Please keep your ritual items separate, and in the container of your choice when not in use. This keeps them sacred and free from unwanted energy.

# Commencing the ritual - Centering

Centering allows you to focus all of your attention on one point, clearing your mind of conscious thoughts so that you can eventually connect with your higher self. Centering takes practice. Just as a marathon runner has to build-up endurance to reach the finish line, centering takes effort before you reach the meditative state. Don't be discouraged if you do not get instant results; remember, everything worthwhile takes practice. Relax and enjoy.

1. Sit comfortably in a quiet environment and close your eyes.
2. Say the following prayer for spiritual protection: ''Dear Father, Mother, God, surround me with your golden, white light of love and protection during my meditation and ritual. All is love and light, all is love and light ... And so it is."

3. Take three or four deep breaths, breathing in through your nose and out through your mouth.
4. Think only of the love and happiness in your life.
5. Fill your mind with a kaleidoscope of vibrant colors, letting them flow into a beautiful sunset or a lush, tropical paradise. Create your own environment
6. Add rewarding personal experiences and all of your life's blessings, i.e., good health, loving partner, good friends, births, graduations, honors, spiritual connections, etc.
7. When your mind is full of these thoughts, bring them down into your heart and let it swell with joy.
8. Visualize your heart turning all of this love and happiness into light which then pours out from your heart into the world for all to see. Feel the experience deeply.
9. Love yourself and be grateful for the gift of love and life. Pass the light to others mentally during this process -- practice this often, it will get easier.

# The Beginning

1. To begin the ritual, bathe or shower in very, warm water. If this is not possible, wash your hands thoroughly with soap and water, (cleansing is symbolic of purification).
2. Pick a quiet place to start, somewhere you feel relaxed and comfortable. Light a white candle, (white is symbolic of purity and protection).
3. Place the burner on a flat, non-flammable surface, i.e., tile, metal or stone. Set the incense in the burner and light.
4. Write your problem on a piece of the special paper, then fold it and put it on the burning incense and light the paper. Hold your touch stone in your right hand (it is your sacred stone), and as the smoke rises, lift your face up to God's infinite universe and read aloud a corresponding affirmation or prayer listed on the following pages.

It is important to initially say the affirmations or prayers out loud because the vibration from the spoken word gives the words power. This spoken power then leads to manifestation.

By saying the words you empower yourself.
By reading the words you empower yourself.
By thinking the words you empower yourself.

This allows you to replace your negative thoughts and feelings with positive vibrations. Take this positive tool and put it into action in your everyday life.

If you feel it is necessary, repeat the affirmation or prayer a second time, or as many times as you wish, until you feel comfortable. By consciously releasing the stress and anxiety from your body, mind and spirit, you will begin the process of healing. While the ashes are cooling, take a few moments to reflect and meditate.

The purification process has begun. BELIEVE. After several hours, when the burner and ashes have thoroughly cooled, decide which of the following methods below would be the most appropriate for the disposal of the remaining ashes.

WATER-FLOW: water keeps things flowing, moving and changing. If you wish something in life to move and flow, place the ashes in a bowl of water for a few minutes, then pour the ashes and water down the sink with the water running over them.

EARTH-GROUNDING: the earth is our foundation, so if you feel a situation needs more stability and foundation, then bury the ashes in the earth for more grounding.

WIND-FREEDOM: the wind stirs things up and whisks them out into the great universe setting them free. If the situation needs more freedom of thought, body or soul, then let the wind carry the ashes out into the world.

If you feel unsure of how you would like to dispose of the ashes at this time, then after they have completely cooled, place them in a container for seven days until you have decided how you wish to dispose of them, (seven days is a sacred waiting period for contemplation and enlightenment before you dispose of the ashes).

For those of you who are unable, or prefer not to use fire in the ritual, visualize your BURNT OFFERINGS igniting, and then burning down into ashes. Then tear the paper into little pieces signifying the burning, and then dispose of the pieces either in the earth, water, or air, just as you would in the fire ritual.

SYMBOL: a sign; an emblem; a type; a figure; an attribute; a creed or summary of religion.

Symbols are a way of triggering or igniting the memory and unlocking past experiences.

As you read the affirmations and prayers, study the symbols; let them sink into your psyche, As you gaze on the symbol at the side of each affirmation and prayer, useful information will come forth into your mind. Write these thoughts down in your journal at the back of the book. BURNT OFFERINGS is the beginning of a wonderful journey for your soul and spirit.

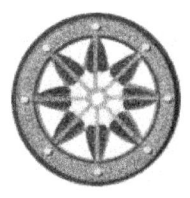

The spiral is the soul's journey of eternal being - life without end.

*Affirmations*: A grouping of positive words, said aloud, that empowers the user to overcome his problems.

# Love

Love is the moving force in my life. It gives me clear eyes to see, open ears to hear, and kind words to speak. Love gives me courage, strength and a complete acceptance of others and myself. Love is my true reality and gives my life its meaning and foundation, moving it forward in a positive and successful way. Love raises my vibration to a higher consciousness. All is love, love is everything.

# Friendship

As I walk my path through life, I will help and befriend people I meet along the way. I will share with them the bonds of honesty, truthfulness, and kindness. I will be there for them physically and emotionally whenever possible. We will celebrate great joys and successes, and we will laugh and cry together as well. I will put a friends' need before my own, knowing these actions epitomize true friendship. I will cherish my friends as I would want to be cherished. And I know, that the love and support of a friend can help me accomplish my goals and realize my dreams. I will truly be blessed by the love of my friends.

# Happiness

*I* greet each new day with awe and excitement, filling my spirit with light and joy. I will laugh and smile sharing my wonder and happiness with people. I will seek those things in life that fill my heart and feed my soul, and I will give thanks for all the gifts I receive each day. I release my worries to a higher power, opening my heart to all the good around me. I project a feeling of well-being and contentment.

# Self-Confidence

As a human being I have everything I need to walk through this world successfully. My good mind and brave heart guide me to find the strength I need in any situation. I am a complete human being and my soul's intuition will bring me clarity in all life's situations. I will radiate kindness and caring to my fellow man. I am confident and poised, perfect and complete.

# Sexuality

As a human being I am also a sexual being, which is healthy and positive. I respect myself as well as others. I love myself knowing that I am a beautiful person, willing to give and receive love equally. I experience sexuality honestly with good intent and a desire to share myself in love. I celebrate this powerful life source with great joy!

# Marriage

My marriage is a complete union of body, mind and spirit. I honor and respect my partner and receive the same back. I will remain an individual, but I will share all I have willingly. I will keep the friendship alive as well as the romance with honesty and kindness, and seek truth and clarity. My marriage is full of love, joy and understanding. Two hearts beating as one.

# Creating a Baby

We open our hearts and our home to let our love create a perfect baby. We pray and know we will have a healthy, happy and contented baby who is bright and learns things easily. Our hearts are open with joy and peace and we will fill the womb with the seed of life.

# Birth of a Baby

When I bring this new life into the world, the birth will be easy, surrounded by the comfort of my family, doctor and nurses. I will put my child's needs before my own and I will use patience and understanding in all situations. I will love and guide this new life to the best of my ability and provide a safe and loving home.

# Success

*I* have the power to create my own success. I can do anything I set my mind to do. I can achieve all my desires and dreams through defining my goals. I will succeed through hard work, diligent research, and networking. I will see what is realistic and work to achieve my success. I will travel all paths of knowledge to succeed. I will succeed!

# Travel

The journey I am to travel will broaden my horizons. The people I meet will enrich my life and give me greater understanding of myself. I will remain safe and comfortable throughout my journey. Let the excitement begin and let the adventure start!

# Universal

I am a wonderful person, healthy, vibrant and happy to be alive. I will make my life the happiest and most successful that I can. I will radiate my love, understanding and patience for all to experience. As a child of God, I know I have a unique destiny all my own, and I will fulfill that destiny with love, compassion and courage.

# Protection

*I* am totally protected by God's, pure, golden, white light. I have no fear of darkness or negativity because I know in my heart and soul that I am safe and secure in love and light. I have everything I need spiritually to protect me and I will walk through this world in the glow of God's perfect aura.

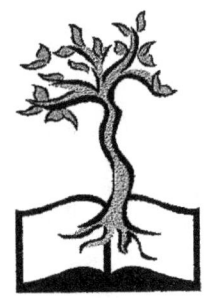

# School & Learning

My mind is open so I can understand and grow with the knowledge before me. I comprehend and store this wisdom for use through my life. I have a clear mind when learning. I am focused and will have a quiet and restful sleep. As I learn, I will share my knowledge by teaching and helping my fellow students. I am on my own path and I know that whatever I need to succeed will be available to me. I will retain all things learned.

# Relationships -- Beginning

Let my heart be opened. I will feel the joy of finding something new about him or her everyday. I will show all the kindness in my heart I have to give, and I will openly accept theirs. I will always respect him or her for the honesty and trust we are sharing. I will always communicate my dreams and desires openly and with love. I will work to bring us closer together while enjoying our independence and uniqueness. All things are possible with love!

# Relationships -- Ending

I will find the strength to overcome this pain of ending my journey with: (person's name). I will be kind and caring, and through this we will grow as individuals. I will continue down my path of life, growing as an individual. I **will** forgive all the pain and problems around this experience. I will move past this situation to a more positive future, growing more and loving myself. I will find the power to overcome and find happiness.

# Deployment of a Loved One

God, I know your arms surround: (person's name) in safety and love. I know their hearts are filled with courage and their minds are clear and think precisely. Their actions will speak louder than words, and there will be no distance between us in spirit. The time will move swiftly and (person's name) will be home safe and sound. The people of the world will be united in the common cause of freedom. We will walk together always in goodness and light.

# Inheritance

Life is the gift, rewards are extra. I will be happy and content with all that comes my way. I will care for the dying and respect their wishes. I will be patient and loving, letting life take care of itself. I will share my reward openly with others. Giving is the greatest gift.

# Wealth

I will achieve financial independence. I completely open myself to all the abundance around me. My mind is open to new opportunities and experiences that will enrich my life as well as others. I have the power to learn all the knowledge put before me. Through wise financial decisions and a steady savings plan I will create a successful future. I will achieve my financial goals!

# Prejudice

As children of the universe we all have the right to be here. I embrace all people, regardless of age, race, creed or color. I respect all their lifestyles and traditions. I consider all people as my brothers and sisters, and I bask in the joy and sensations of a multicultural world. I find delight in the traditions, foods and religions of our universe and I respect all forms of life. I will forgive ignorance and wrap love around others hatreds and prejudices. I will be a light worker for the unity and peace of mankind.

# Religion

I respect all sacred worship. My mind is completely open to different religions, realizing that they all benefit mankind's spiritual nature. I honor the individual's right to choose and practice his or her religion as they see fit. I grow in knowledge and respect for each man's right to choose his own life's path. I will remember that God resides with love in all our hearts and brings us together in the universal consciousness of light and love. All is one under God.

# Loneliness

I am never lonely because the richness of life surrounds me and gives me all 1 need to be whole. I will see the beauty and wonder in and around my life. I will make the effort to join charities and volunteer for causes that I believe in, collecting true friends along the way. I will not be lonely, and my openness and love for others brings the right people to me. They give my life joy and meaning.

# Abuse

I do not accept any physical, mental, verbal or sexual abuse in my life. As a human being, I acknowledge only love, respect and acceptance. My self-esteem will alert me to abuse and enable me to remove myself from it completely. I have a right to walk through my life in peace, safety and dignity. I will be healthy, happy and full of forgiveness.

# Addiction

I admit 1 am addicted to: (addiction). I will use all my strength and power to be stronger than my addiction. I strive to live in reality rather than the half-life of addiction. I will have the courage to overcome my pain and today is the day I take another step forward to a new and better life. Tomorrow I will take another step knowing I have the power to make my goals a reality. I will overcome!

# Eating Disorder

I have the power to overcome my eating disorder. I look at food as natural and healthy, nourishing my body and mind. My body is a miracle worthy of the best food and care I can give it. I exercise with joy knowing it makes me feel better and look healthier. I will respect and love myself for who I am, and my life will be filled with harmony and contentment.

# Aging

From the day of my birth, I have been on the journey to discover myself, growing in the knowledge and understanding of my being. As I walk through this life I will enjoy each day and welcome each birthday as a celebration of life. I understand and accept the wisdom of birth and death and realize that age is not a number, but a growing experience, full of knowledge. No matter where my path takes me I will fill it with the enjoyment of life. My soul is forever young, and my spirit is eternal.

# Surgery

I am giving up my worry knowing I am in caring and knowledgeable hands. I am relaxed and calm and have faith in my higher power, knowing the best results will come forth. I will be healed and free of pain, able to move on with my life in a healthy state of being. I will give myself the time to heal and repair. I will do everything possible to recover fully.

# Losing a Job

My time at: (place of work), has come to an end. I leave with a positive attitude knowing I have gained knowledge and friends. I know when one door closes another one opens, leading me to new horizons. I will seek a job suited to my special talents and interests. I will put all of my assets to work to find a job that fills my personal and monetary needs.

# Personality Conflicts

Giving love comes easy for me. I will think before I speak. I will be honest, direct and kind. With all situations that arise, I will respect the other person as I would like to be respected. My eyes and heart will be open to learn all that is necessary to become a perfect being in harmony with: (person's name). I will surround myself with truth and honesty, and I will expect the same truth and honesty back. I know the laws of cause and effect are always working, so I am always responsible for my actions. I hold my person in the highest regard.

# Guilt

Guilt is a futile emotion that I will release completely. I regret my wrong doings and I will work to undo them. I will speak the truth and expect the truth from others as well. I will create a better world around me that promotes honesty, love and respect. I have learned from my mistakes and I will work to be a stronger and healthier person.

# Shame

I can no longer live in the past. I ask and receive forgiveness for myself and move ahead with my life. I see my mistakes and I will keep growing in strength and happiness, using my love and truth to improve my life and all those who share it. I will release my shame and replace it with light and love. I will move forward into a positive life. I will remove the energy and drama from situations I'm not proud of. I will rise above the challenges that come before me.

# Prayers

**prayer**: a reverent entreaty to God ( a power higher than oneself), to intervene in a worrisome situation.

# Universal Prayer

Dear Father, Mother, God, thank you for all of the abundance and joy in my life. Please give me your love and wisdom to help me through the hard times. Let me find the courage to handle all situations with integrity and compassion, so I can grow into a better human being. Let me learn from my mistakes so that I don't repeat them. Let me forgive my enemies so that I can grow in soul and spirit. Let my life be full of love and light and let me share it generously with all who come my way. As a being of light, I believe in the love that connects mankind together. In this unity of light let us bring forth a connected consciousness of world peace, harmony, love and freedom.

Amen

# Prayer for the Dying

Please Father, Mother, God, I pray through your infinite wisdom and love that the journey to your kingdom will be a quick and painless passing. May the spirit and soul of: (person's name), move into your divine light and be guided by your love and wisdom, to eternal peace and enlightenment. In my mourning, I pray that you soothe my sorrow and lighten my heart so that I can go on in peace and hope. I know that life is eternal and that the soul rises to a higher place of love and learning. We are always safe in your loving embrace.

                                                  Amen

# Prayer for Peace

God, help me to find that place in my heart where love dwells. Let me rise above the problems of the world that I cannot solve, but improve the world around me when I can. Let me reflect deep inside of myself for ways to be kinder to my fellow man, enjoying the diversity of cultures in an atmosphere of tolerance and understanding. Bring me love, patience, compassion and honesty so I can pour them onto the world like a healing balm. Let us work together to rid the world of hate, vengeance and evil, improving the living standards for the less fortunate cultures and countries. Let us aid the sick and dying, and feed the starving people all over the world. Let us move forward in peaceful progress to new enlightenment, awareness and love.

# Spiritual Vocabulary

Enhance your life
with the power of words"

## SAY THE WORDS, AND GAIN THE POWER
*These words and definitions were channeled to Janet during a meditation in 1997.*

AURA: a force-field that takes light from the universal energy in order to surround our bodies, displaying who we are physically, mentally and spiritually using the power of color.

BEAUTY: the loveliness in a person or thing that inspires love and joy in all who behold it.

BLESSINGS: everything in life which is holy and divine that is given as a gift for us to partake and enjoy.

BLISS: a state of perfect happiness that is devoid of all worry and anxiety.

BRILLIANCE: all that is shining and splendid and that comes from the light; the absence of dark; the bright glow that comes from love, beauty and compassion for all things.

COMPASSION: a stage of spiritual growth in which one person is able to feel another's pain and attempt to lesson the intensity of that pain; a deep caring for other people and the ability to put them first.

FAITH: a supreme trust that the laws of the universe will bring answers to questions and solutions to problems; a state of deep knowledge.

GOD: the supreme life force of the universe that holds the ultimate energy, which in turn fuels our body, mind and spirit.

GRACE: an energy that is flowing and divine and one with the universe; to have a feeling of oneness with God; "a state of grace

HARMONY: a feeling of balance brought about by a cooperation between energies that are at peace.

HEALING: a deep love that encompasses our bodies and spirits in order to cure disease and/or unrest; a peaceful power that replaces strife ,which in turn makes us whole.

HONESTY: justness with ourselves and with other people, that gives our lives meaning and quality.

HOPE: a sense of optimism that is based on faith and the understanding of our place in the universe; the knowledge that we always have a future.

JOY: a deep happiness that swells from its roots in the psyche as a result of one's healthy inner life.

LIGHT: the radiant energy that is the source of love and understanding; a weightless energy that lets one ascend and does not bring us down; the glow that is God's aura.

LOVE: all positive feelings and actions we have for ourselves and others; the opposite of fear.

MANIFESTATION: the process of using the powerful, positive energy of ones' mind in order to transform an idea or wish from abstract thought into tangible reality or matter.

PASSION: our deep, strong emotions, fueled by the energy to create the important things in our lives; a caring that goes beyond enthusiasm into the sublime.

RAPTURE: an exalted, trance-like feeling that can place one into a higher state of consciousness in order to connect with God.

STRENGTH: a power within that urges us to be better, more courageous, and more loving regardless of our circumstances; the characteristic of never giving up on life.

STRIVING: the process of struggling which is necessary to fully know and understand ourselves, so that we are able to complete the projects in our lives that nurture growth and elevate our spirits.

TOLERANCE: the ability to know when not to interfere in another persons' situation; the action of allowing others to live their own paths peacefully, learning their own lessons in their own way.

TRUTH: being faithful to your reality and its rules of conduct; an understanding of all that is genuine in your life and following it.

UNDERSTANDING: the use of our compassion and intelligence to fully understand another person or situation in the right light.

# Self-Help Suggestions

# Addiction

1. Once you have admitted to an addiction, seek professional help.
2. Make changes in your friends and surroundings, eliminating the ones that contribute to your problem.
3. Reward yourself when you succeed.
4. Look into a 12-step program.
5. Join a support group - it helps to have company.
6. Only talk about your addiction with people you trust.
7. Use local hot lines in your city — they are free and there to help.
8. Look into the hidden reasons for your behavior through a counselor of your choice — this can speed-up the healing process.
9. Seek a spiritual counselor of your choice to give you hope and strength.

# Aging

1. Keep fit mentally and physically.
2. Take vitamins, exercise and eat well.
3. Laugh a lot — it's good for anything that ails yah!
4. Enjoy the self-confidence that your years have brought you.
5. Enjoy young friends and family and see their point of view as well.
6. Save for retirement so you can relax.
7. Improve your looks if it makes you feel better.
8. Be realistic and don't get caught in the "age trap" - you really are as young as you feel.
9. Think young and progressively.
10. Don't ever let your inner child grow-up.
11. Use prayer and meditation to connect to a higher consciousness so that you stay in a state of light and love.

# Birth of a Baby

1. Educate yourself on the birthing process by taking a class, reading books, and watching instructional videos.
2. Have a plan in place before your delivery due date to eliminate chaos.
3. Make all your desires known for your delivery, i.e., type of anesthetic, natural childbirth, who will be in the delivery room with you, etc.
4. Pick the child's name before the birth.
5. Pick someone you're comfortable with to help after the birth for at least the first few weeks.
6. Prepare a nursery with all the practical needs.
7. Be prepared for some depression after the delivery it's common with many women and doesn't last too long.
8. Feel and savor the happiness and joy of this wonderful occasion.

# Creating a Baby

1. Both partners should have a positive frame of mind.
2. Both should have a complete physical check-up.
3. Prepare financially - be realistic.
4. Eat healthy foods from all the food groups to eliminate any deficiency in the body.
5. Don't drink alcohol, smoke or take drugs (unless prescribed by your doctor).
6. Exercise sensibly — too much strenuous exercise sometimes can inhibit fertility.
7. Keep a normal body weight - being too thin can also inhibit fertility.
8. Be romantic, laugh, relax and be happy.

# Deployment of a Loved One

1. Get all legal papers in order such as wills, power of attorney's and insurance policies, so that in case of an emergency things will run smoothly.
2. Know your rights as a citizen and a relative of the deployed person — many government benefits are available to you in this situation.
3. Express your feelings of love to the one deployed before they leave so that they carry the love with them and you have no regrets.
4. Form a support group of loving people who can help you with any feelings of loneliness and fear; this will ease the pain and panic.
5. Use all available communication (phone, letters, email, etc.) to connect with this person; this keeps their spirits up as well as yours.
6. Pray and meditate daily for spiritual solace.
7. Talk to a spiritual advisor from your faith to relieve some of the burden and to lighten your spirit.

# Eating Disorder

1. Once you admit you have an eating disorder, seek reputable, professional help to find out the core reason, and set-up a program you can realistically follow.
2. Be around people who you trust and who want you to succeed.
3. Find a realistic picture of someone you admire and strive for that image and not for something you can't attain.
4. Take each day at a time.
5. Learn to look at food as a friend and not an enemy. Remember that it fuels our bodies, just like gasoline fuels our cars. It is necessary to our well-being.
6. "Know thyself" is the first step to positive change. Find out what the motivating force is in your life. This will empower you.
7. Don't compare yourself to other people — you are unique.
8. Make a list of all the good things about yourself, physically, emotionally, mentally and spiritually. Dwell on these attributes everyday until they become your mantra.
9. Get your mind off of yourself and your physical image and talk to people about their hopes and fears; this makes you a more interesting person and much more likeable.

# Friendship

1. Be open and willing to accept other people as friends.
2. Choose friends wisely according to your value system.
3. Accept a friend's faults as you would expect them to accept yours.
4. Be a good listener, and be kind and honest with your suggestions and advice.
5. Keep in contact either by phone, email or visits to establish an enduring friendship.
6. Once in a while tell friends that you love them — it's so nice to hear.
7. When a friend tells you something in strict confidence, respect their wishes and keep their secret.
8. Once in a while, surprise a friend with a thoughtful gift to show that you are thinking of them.

# Guilt

1. Look into yourself to make sure you're not taking on guilt you don't deserve.
2. If you have made a mistake, admit it and try to remedy the situation.
3. Consciously take responsibility for a mistake and say I'm sorry, out loud and sincerely.
4. Talk to a spiritual advisor or therapist about your motives and whether they're pure or not.
5. Use prayer to ask for divine guidance and forgiveness — this will help to ease the stress and bring you some needed answers.

# Happiness

1. Make a list of all the things that make you happy, then pick two or three things and work on them.
2. Smile at people and greet them warmly — they usually respond in kind.
3. Dwell on the positive things in your life — try to put the negative things in perspective and don't dwell on them.
4. Try to be around happy people - it will rub off.
5. Take up a new challenge such as:
    a) going back to school
    b) enrolling in an art or dance class (it's joyful).
    c) learn a new sport
    d) redecorate your living space (surroundings make a difference).
    e) read uplifting books and watch funny movies.
6. Give to those less fortunate and you will realize how lucky you are with what you have.
7. Balance your life - too much of anything can create stress, leading to depression.

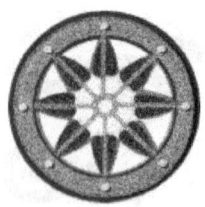

# Inheritance

1. Make wills and trusts out to follow your wishes
   — no mistakes.
2. Don't fight over things like dogs over a bone
   — come to agreements in a calm manner.
3. If there are problems, hire a good lawyer to sort it all out.
4. Understand that inheritance is a gift, not a sure thing.
5. Take emotions into consideration and don't talk about inheritances at the funeral.
6. Remember the dead with kindness and love.
7. If things don't go your way completely, accept and move on with your life - if you don't, you only hurt yourself.
8. Don't live your life counting on an inheritance that might not materialize.

# Loneliness

1. Push yourself to call friends.
2. Fill your calendar in advance and have positive things to look forward to.
3. Take a class to meet nice people with the same interests.
4. Invite people over for dinner and extend yourself more.
5. Baby-sit for children
   — they accept you just the way you are.
6. Plant a garden
   — it's a wonderful way to connect with God.
7. Look inside yourself and make a friend of yourself.
8. Join a gym or a church group.
9. Get active in charities
   — there's always someone who needs you.
10. Think more about other people and their problems
    — this takes you away from yours.

# Losing a Job

1. When you are informed of the lay-off, talk to Human Resources and find out about what is owed to you, such as: severance pay, 401 k's, vacation pay, matched asset plans, sick pay, extended health insurance (COBRA), etc.
2. Don't panic, stay calm and focused; this way you won't miss any opportunities that could be around you.
3. Talk to good friends and family about your feelings and fears to get them out in the open; this way they won't turn into depression.
4. Contact your local unemployment agency and sign-up as soon as possible for your benefits, since there's usually a two week waiting period.
5. Update your resume and contact a job search firm who charges the corporation a fee and not you; they can do most of the legwork for you and cut down on your stress.
6. If you have done work favors for other people in the past, don't hesitate to call them for a return favor. You would be amazed at how well this works sometimes.
7. Find out if there was something you weren't doing right on the lost job and fix it for the next one; this can only help you in the long run.

8. If you need to update your skills, take advantage of low-fee night school or ask skilled friends to give you a few hours of their time — people usually like to help someone who is sincere about learning and bettering themselves
9. Don't beat yourself up — many highly, successful people have been fired, laid-off, or rejected for a job. Think of it as an opportunity to learn new things and meet new people.
10. Ask for spiritual help; prayers and meditation relieve stress and no sincere plea goes unheard.

# Love

1. Love yourself and the rest will follow.
2. Be kind and caring of others' needs and feelings.
3. Offer your assistance to someone in need
   — this is a special kind of love.
4. Let love grow like a beautiful garden
   — give it time to blossom.
5. Talk about loving feelings with people you love and trust
   — they like to hear from you.
6. Don't let every little thing bother you, this is a sure way to kill love.
7. Give a gift for no special reason.
8. Act more romantic and playful and laugh.
9. Don't let yourself be used or abused, only loved.
10. Respect is an important aspect of love.
11. Live love, don't just talk about it.
12. Possessiveness is not love, it's a prison
    — don't go there.
13. Tell others you love them - it's the nicest gift.

# Marriage

1. Get to know the person well before you marry them.
2. Be friends first.
3. Understand their needs and desires.
4. State your needs and desires, such as money, joint accounts, children, etc.
5. Help each other to succeed.
6. Talk to each other sincerely.
7. Act honestly — if you're unhappy about something, speak-up respectfully.
8. Don't put the other person down.
9. Seek therapy if things seem out of control.
10. Do not cheat on your mate.
11. If you have outgrown the marriage, think of ways to save it, or move on honestly and kindly.
12. Don't let other people get involved in the inner workings of your marriage.
13. Always consider the well-being of your children.
14. Perform loving and giving acts for others - this cements the love.

# Personality Conflicts

1. Honestly ask yourself which person is the real problem.
2. Take a good look at both sides.
3. Stay calm and talk it out as soon as possible.
4. Treat the other person as you would like to be treated.
5. If talking doesn't work, write a letter explaining your side.
6. Don't push the other person's buttons.
7. Don't talk behind their back and play games.
8. Learn to say, "I'm sorry, it's my fault," if it is.
9. Learn to forgive, everyone makes mistakes.
10. Always be truthful and don't change the circumstances to fit your own needs.
11. Don't resort to violence or any other kind of abuse.
12. Allow a few days to pass and then think about whether another conversation is necessary. Think about whether the matter can be resolved.
13. If the other person is abusive and continues to argue, just walk away and say nothing until you're calm.
14. Grow from each experience and learn from your mistakes and theirs.

# Prejudice

1. Educate yourself on different races and religions.
2. Expand your mind to realize that we have a variety of races and creeds because we need to.
3. If you can't accept someone or something, move away from them and leave them alone — as long as it does not harm anyone or anything, it has a right to be here as well.
4. Try foreign foods and music to broaden your life - the variety is truly a gift.
5. Remember that there will always be someone prejudiced against you as well - none of us is exempt from this blight.
6. Don't voice prejudice thoughts — they are better left unsaid, in any circumstances.

# Provisions for the Dying

1. Have a will or living trust to make sure everything goes to the right people and places.
2. Specifically detail the people you want to have cherished objects - this prevents misunderstandings.
3. Make your wishes known about your burial arrangements in writing.
4. Have the people around you who give you love and comfort; this helps you, and them at the same time.
5. Contact a clergy of your choice; let your spiritual life take care of you.
6. If there is time and strength, do some of the things you always wanted to do and didn't.
7. Make peace with yourself and your enemies; this is a freeing experience.
8. Talk about the good things in your life with friends and loved ones so that they have memories clear in their hearts and minds.

# Protection

1. Light a white candle and burn sage to clear your environment of any negativity.
2. Meditate and pray to keep your mind and spirit positive and full of light.
3. Stay away from people who give off dark or negative energy; they will drain your psyche and bring you down.
4. Don't dabble with the dark side; it will only bring you darkness and chaos.
5. If you feel any darkness around you, ask the Archangel Michael to protect you and surround you in God's holy, white light.

# Relationships — Beginning

1. Smile and be warm and friendly - this brings people close to you.
2. Say hello to people who return your gaze.
3. While standing near someone who you think is attractive, start a conversation.
4. Be a good listener - this is an attractive asset.
5. Carry yourself straight and with confidence.
6. Know what attributes you're looking for before you begin.
7. Make a friend first, then let the relationship build naturally.
8. Look for someone who shares your goals, morals and beliefs.
9. Looks aren't everything - people skills are.
10. Be honest with your feelings and trust other people unless there is a good reason not to.
11. Treat others as you would like to be treated.
12. If you decide to have sex, always be protected.

# Relationships — Ending

1. Don't break-up until you have weighed all the consequences; compulsive behavior can ruin your life.
2. Don't play games - end a relationship because you know it's over and you need to move on with your life.
3. Show respect to the other person and try not to hurt them needlessly.
4. If there are children involved, make sure they know they are loved and not responsible for the break-up.
5. Get counseling together and apart, and show respect.
6. Talk to friends and loved ones you can trust — they will have your well-being at heart.
7. Stay busy and go out with friends and co-workers for some fun.
8. Take up a sport or sign-up at a gym or take classes for self-improvement and relaxation.
9. Don't think of what could have been, think of what is - reality is much better than self-delusion.
10. Don't have unprotected, random sex - this could make your situation much worse in the long run.

# School and Learning

1. Look into yourself and find the talents you can use to your benefit.
2. With these talents and gifts, find a field in which you can succeed.
3. Research your choices by looking into the school's programs, years of study and the costs.
4. Research funding, loans, grants and scholarships, as well as loans from your parents if they have the money.
5. Talk to people who are already successful in your field of study and find out about the pay, bonuses, working conditions, etc.
6. Be organized, do your homework, utilize the library and get a computer.
7. Enjoy learning and make it more fun than a burden.

# Self-Confidence

1. Make a list of all your attributes.
2. Look in the mirror and see your beauty.
3. Be honest, kind and loving to yourself.
4. Ask others that you trust, how they see you.
5. Face your weaknesses and improve on them.
6. Seek counseling if needed.
7. Pick a challenge, tackle it, and succeed at it to build self-esteem.
8. Learn something new and educate yourself.
9. Take up a physical challenge to get yourself going
10. Meditate, using either yoga, Tai Chi, or pray.
11. Think realistically and change things about yourself that you can.
12. Relax and lighten-up.
13. Think happy thoughts about yourself and your life — it's much better than the alternative.

# Sexuality

1. Know yourself.
2. Respect yourself.
3. Respect others.
4. Understand what turns you on.
5. Know your boundaries and where you will and will not go.
6. Don't judge others' lifestyles
    — it serves no good purpose.
7. If you're sexually active, get tested every six months.
8. Develop your own personality.
9. Give and receive affection openly.
10. Dress appropriately
    — be clean and well-groomed; express your personality.
11. Don't assume anything.
12. Talk openly about your desires and concerns with your partner.
13. Be truthful about your expectations and desires.

# Shame

1. Do not live in the past.
2. If you were at fault ask for forgiveness, say you're sorry and mean it.
3. If you sincerely try to right a wrong and it isn't accepted, don't beat yourself up forever ~ that's futile.
4. Get therapy or counseling to move you through the pain.
5. Get medical treatment if necessary for stress-related problems tied to the shame.
6. Seek spiritual help from a priest, rabbi, minister, lama, etc. Sometimes we need a higher power to take over the burden.

# Success

1. Read everything about someone who is in your chosen field so you can find out how they succeeded.
2. Choose a few small goals and attain them before tackling the big ones.
3. Take advantage of inexpensive, adult education courses to learn all you can about your subject.
4. Ask for help — most people like to help someone who's willing to learn.
5. Be more assertive about reaching your goals by using enthusiasm and joy in your everyday life.
6. Success is different to everyone - make sure you know what it means to you personally.
7. Surround yourself with confident people who are traveling the road to success.

# Surgery

1. Always get a least two doctor's opinions; don't reveal the first doctor's diagnosis to the second doctor to see if they match.
2. When you pick a doctor, check his credentials with the American Medical Association for any history of malpractice, etc.
3. Ask each doctor for his recommendations for treatment, cost, recovery time, and hospital stay.
4. Talk to other people who have had the same surgery.
5. Make sure you know your insurance and disability options.
6. Let pain be your guide.
7. Look into alternative medicine such as acupuncture, herbal therapy, etc., to speed your recovery.
8. Read all that you can on the subject and be informed of the risks.
9. Get all the rest you need and don't go back to work too soon.
10. Have your business in order such as wills, trusts, etc., just in case the worst arises.
11. Don't worry, it never solved anything.
12. Use prayer and meditation to connect with the Universal spirit of love.
13. Think positively!

# Travel

1. Create positive excitement by gathering brochures from a travel agency on your destination, so you feel prepared.
2. Prepare all of your arrangements well in advance so you can relax.
3. Rent travel videos to watch at home to feel involved with your destination.
4. Buy a good, easy-to-read translation book if you are traveling to a country that speaks a foreign language.
5. If you are nervous and fearful of flying, take some classes in deep breathing and meditation - these will help you to stay calm.
6. If you cannot control your fear through breathing and meditation, ask your doctor for a suitable medication to help you to get through the journey.
7. Tell the flight attendant at the beginning of the flight if you have fear problems with flying, so she can be aware and more available to you if you need help

# Universal

1. Upon waking, take time to truly savor the ordinary things around you such as:
    a) the feel of the warm shower on your body.
    b) the sound of the birds singing outside.
    c) the taste of your breakfast food and drink.
    d) the smell of the morning air.
2. During your day do something nice for yourself and someone else - no matter how small it is, it will make a difference.
3. Set aside a few minutes of quiet time during your day to just center yourself, be still and meditate.
4. When going to bed at the end of the day, breathe deeply and release the worries of the day as you would release a bird up into the sky.
5. Give thanks for your life and all the people in it.
6. Ask God for protection and a deep peaceful sleep

# Wealth

1. Think of an idea you feel comfortable with, then make a marketing plan and present it to a bank for a business loan.
2. Write stories, articles and books on subjects you know well and sell them.
3. Take a sum of money and invest it wisely in the stock market.
4. Save some money every month, even a small amount - it will eventually grow.
5. Circulate with successful, wealthy people to network, exchange ideas and cement friendships and relationships.
6. Share living expenses with a room-mate.
7. Save coupons and money-back forms.
8. Know your means and don't overspend.
9. Trade services with friends; turn a hobby into cash and sell items that you make yourself.
10. Buy inexpensive real estate and fix it up yourself.
11. Manage property for free rent.
12. Share child care expenses with friends and family,.
13. Take advantage of public schools and colleges for low tuition fees.

"Man's soul is too revered by God to let it die; the soul becomes spirit that is eternal."

# THE POWER OF SYMBOLS

Symbolism gives relevance to all that we hold sacred as human beings. They are evident in the emblems we wear, the logos on our businesses, and the carvings on our stones and monuments.

Symbols are a visual connection that unlock doors to the subconscious by triggering remembrances of past life experiences, and important events that can bring clarity into your present life. A symbol can evoke many associated meanings, each in its way, a marker leading us to a better understanding of where we've been and were we want to go.

Carl Gustav Jung, the eminent psychiatrist, knew that symbols were significant in reaching the subconscious for clues to a patient's memories and repressed desires. This method is still successfully used today in modern Jungian therapy.

The order in which you read these symbols is important; always start with the symbol of Fire, then ascend through each symbol until you reach the Phoenix. These symbols are lamp posts along your way; STARE AT THEM, MEDITATE ON THEM, feel them emotionally and psychically. By charting the information you receive from these symbols, you will evoke inner memories and bring clarity into your present life.

They can connect you with your spiritual center, help you to manifest solutions to problems, and give birth to your dreams.

Your journal is a way of charting your progression through problems, your spiritual experiences, and the knowledge and wisdom you gain, as well as the personal symbols revealed to you along your journey.

It would be helpful to list the dates of your rituals along with the corresponding questions, and the dates of any changes or shifts that occur. This will allow you to see any patterns or anomalies that would be helpful to your growth.

*Fire* symbolizes the purification of the soul, bringing forward needed information.

### Book
symbolizes the quest for knowledge, wisdom and enlightenment.

$\mathcal{S}$unflower
symbolizes reaching loftier solutions to problems by rising above them and overcoming ego for clarity.

## Sun

represents the inner power; universal source of light and energy; life-giving force.

## Wheel of life

symbolizes the infinite possibilities, eternal life, and perpetual motion.

# Eye of Horus

Represents seeing clearly, protection, and a perfect understanding of what is; reality.

# Phoenix

represents a symbolic renewal and rebirth of greater opportunities from the ashes — purification and new life.

www.ingramcontent.com/pod-product-compliance
Lightning Source LLC
Chambersburg PA
CBHW071956070426
42453CB00008BA/833